NIGHT DRIVING

Poetry for Life's Journey

By

Reginald O. Johns

ISBN: 1-4140-3684-1 (e-book)
ISBN: 1-4140-3683-3 (Paperback)

This book is printed on acid free paper.

For book signings and direction on booking Reginald O. Johns for
poetry readings-email:reginaldjohns@hotmail.com

Reprinted poems are quoted from **CHOICES *Poetry for a Positive
Direction***. Used by permission.

1stBooks - rev. 11/11/03

ACKNOWLEDGMENTS...

I give many thanks to Elizabeth White. As my editor, you are superb; as my friend, you are divine. With each submission, I anxiously await what your pencil will speak. Your words inspire me to reflect and acknowledge God's gifting in me. Thank you for sharpening me like iron.

I also give thanks to my wonderful parents, Harold and Marion Johns. Your words and support have been an enormous source of encouragement. May God richly bless you for your wonderful stewardship as parents.

ACKNOWLEDGEMENTS

DEDICATION...

I dedicate this work to the Holy Spirit. Your consistent voice of encouragement and exhortation stirs me to be all I can be. Your words have always lifted me to dream, believe, follow you, and receive the best God has for me.

CONTENTS...

FILLING UP

THE CALL

I look to Jesus
Who bids me to come

Walk upon the water
To the sure foundation

The Word of God
Tested, tried, and true

Yes, Lord Jesus
I believe you

And will faithfully complete
The task you have

Given me
to do

Reginald O. Johns

HOW?

How can I do this
How can I overcome
The Holy Ghost shall come upon you
Sent by the Son

How shall I do this
How shall it be done
The Holy Ghost shall come upon you
Sent by the Son

How shall I do this
How can it be for me
The Holy Spirit that is upon you
Witnesses I'm with thee

As you have spoken
Let it also be done
I receive the Spirit of the Father
Sent by His Son

ALL THAT I HAVE...

All that I have is thine
The Father said to the faithful son

All that I have is thine
Was said to him who did not run

All that I have is thine
Belonged to him who stayed

In the house of his father
Whose word he obeyed

Reginald O. Johns

JUST ASK

One can only be greedy
If there is a limited supply

Who would care if you took 2 slices
From a million available pies

As you approach God's throne
Remember He is not man

He has abundant resources
Within the palm of His hands

That are long enough
To reach you and pick you up

Supply abundantly your needs
And overflow your cup

LOVE IS A GIVER

Love is a giver
He gives to me
Beyond my basic needs
To survive daily

Love is a giver
He gives to me
The requests of my lips
I am full and happy

Love is a giver
He gives to me
The desires of my heart
I have abundantly

Love is a giver
Love gives to me
For this one reason
Love loves me

THE MAP

THE GIFT

Hands gave it to you
This you did not earn

Hands gave it to you
Now it's time to learn

About this gifting
That's been imparted to you

How to operate it
And benefit from its use

Hands gave it to you
With His good intentions

Follow those hands to His heart
Receive His direction

Reginald O. Johns

PURPOSE

If I told you everything
Would you believe

The mighty plan
I have for thee

I tell you in part
By a prophet or a dream

So you would search out my Word
To find stones in a stream

To sling at Goliaths
That try to psyche you out

With their words of unbelief
Profanity and doubt

Behind my Word
I put my power

To slay your Goliaths
This very hour

Get ready, practice
With your stones

Your strength comes from me
Your God alone

Read my Word
Worship and sing

And I will continue
To unveil my Son in thee

CONCEPTION

Keep believing
the words
I've given you

They are the keys
That will unlock
My future for you

Thoughts that are good
To fulfill the expected end

Plans of life that unfold
From deep within

Wasn't your being
Created from a seed

That took time to develop
Once a woman had conceived

For a God that's eternal
Nine months is nothing

Neither is the time I take
To bring your vision into being

Reginald O. Johns

HOLDFAST

Holdfast to sound words
Words that make sense

Let not go of wisdom
Once it has been dispensed

Buy the truth, sell it not
For large sums of cash

Foundations of truth always remain
Storms always pass

TRUTH

Dreams don't come true
They already are
In the soul, in the mind
And even the heart

Dreams become apparent
For others to see
They are already true
To those who believe

16

REST AREAS

PASTOR

He held me close
And did not let go
After prayer

But instead
Drew
Me closer

He held me
Though I looked fine

After he prayed
He took time

And held me
Like my daddy

And I sighed deeply
And was carried beyond weary

Into hope

Reginald O. Johns

BISHOP JOHN AND PASTOR ANNE GIMENEZ

His eyes were the sky
Inviting me to fly
and believe

Her hands were fire
Imparting an inward desire
To be faithful and holy

NIGHT DRIVING

When driving in the dark
It does not trouble my heart
Only to see the road before me

With confidence I glide
To the other side
To reach destinations I desire to be

But in my drive of faith
Sometimes I have to wait
And frustrations seem to find me

but
A light to my path
A lamp to my feet
His word provides for me

So, I'll take His peace
He's given to me
And rest in the midst of the storm

Stay on the path
Do what He asks
When things are not the norm

Reginald O. Johns

REST

He made me lie down
Because I refused to rest

Coerced me to drink living water
As I laid upon His breast

And just then
It began to overflow

Thanksgiving and gratitude
For the Savior I know

He made me lie down
On pastures of green

And led me to drink
From a still, fulfilling stream

And see beyond
What I can do for Him

And be strengthened
In the inner man

Whom He is
interested in

THE MAN IN PINK

She said you wore pink
The day she met you
Sitting under a tree

And she came closer
As more than an observer
To cast her cares upon thee

And saw a sparkling white robe
That glistened and glowed
With all the colors of the rainbow

She confessed her deep fears
To you who hears
And strengthens in times of sorrow

Felt hands that were warm
For healing ones torn
And broken in their heart

You stroked her brown hair
Promised to be there
When she was afraid of the dark

Though several years old
Was this story when told
An account of seeing the Savior

I received it as truth
As something you would do
For your child who was in danger

ACCELERATE

NO ASPHALT NEEDED

Don't look
For others to show you the way

Use your feet
To trod the way

Tread down high grasses
And make a path

Be not dismayed
By unbelievers who snicker and laugh

What I have for you
Will move you beyond a position of rest

A fulfillment of dreams
That makes Christ manifest

Reginald O. Johns

CONFRONTATION

Face the dark
As if you are
Surrounded by light

Let not your
Heart be troubled
By shadows in the night

For, "Let there be"
Creates stars in the universe

Intense enough to enlighten planets
And support life on the Earth

THE MATCH

After Jacob wrestled with the angel
I know he had to rest
When you're wrestling with God
You're wrestling with the best

A God unyielding with power
Infinite, holy, divine
Knowing all the tricks of procrastination
That steal His precious time

Never changing His direction
Purpose, nor plan
Waiting for us to surrender
To the control of His hand

Able to stand His ground
Unyielding by a bribe
The promises we make
If he would come to our side

Yet, merciful enough that
Our spirits He does not crush
Who knows without a doubt
It's His will or bust

Put down your hitch-hiking finger
You can't get away
Labor to enter into His rest
Choose to obey

DETOURS AHEAD

DEAD END

You might see
This thing as finished
But I know the end

You might see
Your life as over
But I'm seeing it begin

To move you
Where I want you

To move you
Where I need you

To move you
To become

Whom I made you
To be

Reginald O. Johns

NEW LAND

When you've been asked
To do something new

Before you say no
Let me give you this clue

God gives land
Not only by titled deed

But by the steps you take
With the soles of your feet

This little opportunity
Is given for your expansion

It is just one of your plots
In the land of Canaan

TRUST

When David was driven
Into the wilderness
He could not go back

When Saul sought
To destroy him
He couldn't retrace his tracks

He had to run
Seek shelter, and hide
Despite the prophetic word
He held onto inside

When Jesus hung on the cross
He could not come down
Despite His innocence
And good works abound

He had to wait and trust
His Father to keep His Word
Raise Him from the dead
Believe what the prophets had heard

CUSTOM DETAILING

A TRIP

Leather seats
Air conditioning
And power steering

Automatic tinted windows
Mirrors
For our steering

Wood grain
Dashboards
Seats that tilt back

Surround Sound
CD players
Pumping music tracks

Once luxuries
Now necessities
Built to our specification

Still not enough to soothe
Spirits of anticipation

Unwilling to enjoy
A journey slower than a jet

But repeatedly in frustration cry
Are we there yet?

Reginald O. Johns

HERE'S MY NUMBER

We have
Secretaries, busy signals
Caller ID, Call waiting
Private lines, unlisted numbers
Who are we imitating?

When we don't want
to be bothered
We can screen and ignore
Those trying to reach us
Whose conversation we abhor

But
Our Father gave us Jesus
So He could easily be reached
And we attribute status
To men who must be beeped

A King so important
Yet He takes His precious time
To always be available
When we get on the line

And call His name
Whether in want or need
Perhaps we're not as important
As we pretend to be

PARENTS

Don't let teachers
Steal your children
From you they should learn

Don't let teachers
Steal your children
From you they should yearn

For knowledge,
Wisdom and wonder

Don't allow teachers to
Steal them from under

your faith and guidance
Don't let them stray

Remember
Pied Pipers only need a beat
To dance children away

CAR WASH

DIRT

Dirt creeps up on you
Rubs on and falls
Right up next to you
It wants to become your all

Dirt creeps up on you
Its beginnings are invisible
Left there all day
Its effects are impenetrable

Under arms not washed
Create forcefields of stink
Keeping loved ones at a distance
Until we reach the sink

To lather and wash
With a handy detergent soap
Like God's Word cleanses our spirits
Enabling us to cope

In a world that is so dirty
We can always get clean
Before our sins become apparent
For everyone to see

Reginald O. Johns

THE SECRET

There must be
Healing in it
Because it is often stopped

By the onlooker
The disciplinarian
Who won't open a heart

To feel the hurt

Suck it up
Shut it up
We tell children and men

But what if tears
Soften clay
And help broken hearts mend

That have been shattered
by the pressure
of unmet expectations

Repairing fractured images of
the God of our salvation

Maybe tears bring cleansing
With sorrow and godly repentance

Making hearts flexible and able
To get up and love again

Salt lowers the temperature
Water is allowed to freeze

Perhaps it does the same for our hearts
Keeping it hopeful, forgiving, and free

INFLUENCES

When I was young
It was my mother
Who made me daily bathe

When I was young
It was my father
Who made me want to behave

When I was young
It was my teacher
Who made me read and learn

When I was young
it was debt
That made me work and earn

Now I am old
It is desire
for the best in life

To cultivate
myself and grow
In God's image day and night

An image
that is holy
Obedient, wise, and wealthy

An image
that makes me
Honest, hardworking, honorable, and healthy

GREEN LIGHTS

EXODUS

When I go
I will not go empty
But with the spoils
Of my enemy

Jewels of gold
Vessels of silver
I shall put
On my sons and daughters

I have favor in the
Sight of the Egyptians
God brings me out
From under their burdens

Into a land
He's promised to me
A land that flows
With milk and honey

Reginald O. Johns

THE MARK

Stop counting the days
Start counting the ways
Share your love today

Stop losing sleep
Looking under trees
For something bought for thee

The greater one gives
The lesser one lives
For someone else to be benevolent

The servant's the king
For his heart can esteem
The value in being compassionate

From Sunday to Monday
Love should overflow
From the 25th to the 26th
Let it seep through and go

Into days not marked with Xs
Which are easy to recognize
But onto days that appear blank
Under the daily disguise

Of numbers we count
To reach another day
Stop
Mark it
With God's love
In your own way

DAILY, I LOVE YOU

Taffy is for Tuesday
If you're feeling blue

Let's have a weekend on Wednesday
If you can't make it through

I'll bring you flowers
For Friday

We'll appreciate God's creation
My love needs not holidays

To be put into activation

RED LIGHTS

ACCOUNTS

Working for retirement
That's what some do

Working for retirement
Is a work for fools

One barn, two barns
Filled with supply

Isn't what I work for
Money's not God Most High

My father's got a business
And a job for me to do

To fulfill His divine purpose
Not live for pleasure like a fool

A man's life consists
Not in abundance that's possessed

An account for my days
I will have to confess

To God

SHINING STARS

Judy wasn't Dorothy
Archibald wasn't Cary
Norma Gene wasn't Marilyn
So
I'll resolve to be me

Why waste hours on make-up
Millions on diamonds
Acquire five wives
And not be content within?
Why spend days on therapy
Take trips with LSD
Hide under black wigs
Or gulp sleeping pills for zzzs?

I can already sleep
I like my own hair
I can drive myself
Don't need drugs to take me there

Change your destination
Don't be the next shooting star
Keep yourself grounded
Shine where you are!

RICH MAN, POOR MAN

The end is more important
Than the beginning

A hot commodity's in your hand
So watch how you're spending

Your days

There's no rewind button
No delete key
Words spoken, deeds done
Last an eternity

A rich man once stepped over a beggar
And never stopped to think
Of the poor in his life
Until he needed a drink

His stock had crashed
His wealth wasn't worth a cent
Spending eternal days
In hell where his soul was sent

NEEDS

Paper and pen
What a combination
Checks and money orders
Covering the needs of a nation
How much is your need?
How big is your debt?
Tell me what you want
So I don't have to get
INVOLVED

Did your mother send a check
When she heard you cry
Or did she leave the kitchen
And make her way outside
To wipe your tears, calm your fears
And kiss the pain away
Some needs don't require checks
But servants who say,
"Send me."

FLAT TIRES

SKELETON

I won't leave you
I'll wait until you're ready
I'm here for you to lean upon
I make your steps steady
I'm committed to you
Even when you fall
Like the bones inside of you
I am your all in all
Jesus

Reginald O. Johns

THE HUGGER

Like quotation marks you hug me
Enclosing me inside
The Alpha-Omega
On both of my sides
To the right and left of me
There is a God said
A rock is my pillow
For me to rest my head
When others go for the soft
I'll stick with the firm
Take up my cross and follow You
From Your Word I'll learn
Lord Jesus Christ

REPENTANCE

I still have a chance
To learn
To try
And succeed

I still have a chance
To repent
Renew
and receive

the life
God has for me

Reginald O. Johns

EVERLASTING GLORY

When my days are old
And my hair is white

My glory shall not be
In strength nor might

But in character
That goes down deep

A nature of God
For all to see

When my years have passed
And my beauty fades

My glory shall not be
In the size of my waist

But in pearls of wisdom
Dispensed from my heart

Cultured from a life with Jesus
With whom I have walked

CHECKERED FLAGS

AND THE WINNER IS...

Heaven has no consolation prize
For those deciding to quit

No year supply of rice
For faith that doesn't stick

In a world of absolutes
There's still abundant grace

That can pick you up
And empower you

To finish
Your fight of faith

THE WINNERS' CIRCLE

CEMENTED FOOTSTEPS

When you've
Made it to the top
Planted your flag and looked down

Forget not the
Old acquaintances
You've left on the ground

The trails you leave
Can't be made of
of dried bread crust

To pave a road to success
Cemented footsteps
Are a must

Share your adventure with others
So they too
Can get going

Who said
Being at the top
Had to be lonely

ABOUT THE AUTHOR

Reginald O. Johns is a native of Hampton, Virginia. He works as an educator in the public schools and is extensively involved in his church and community. His first publication, **CHOICES: Poetry for a Positive Direction** was a compilation of many poetic styles which magnified beauty like a sculpture for others to appreciate and ponder.